**Doncaster**
Metropolitan Borough Council

**DONCASTER LIBRARY AND INFORMATION SERVICES**
www.doncaster.gov.uk

Please return/renew this item by the
last date shown.
Thank you for using your library.

InPress 0231 June 09

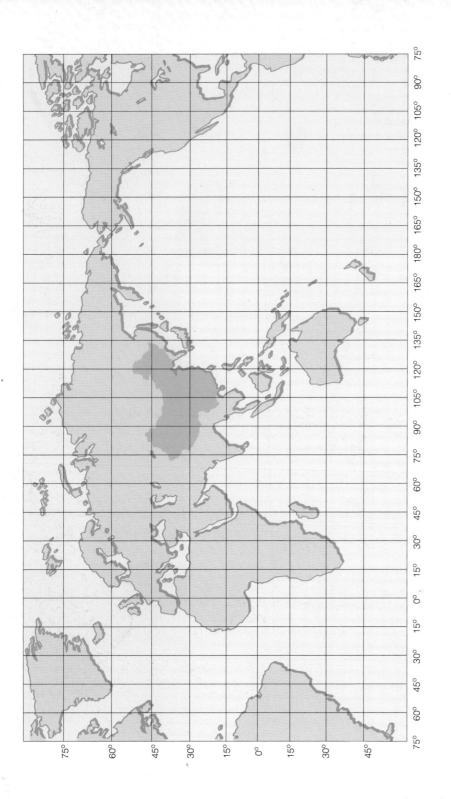

**In addition to China's 22 provinces, there are:**

**5 AUTONOMOUS REGIONS**

NEI MONGGOL (Inner Mongolia)

XIZANG (Tibet)

XINJIANG

GUANGXI

NINGXIA

**1 SPECIAL ADMINISTRATIVE REGION**

HONG KONG

**4 MUNICIPALITIES**

BEIJING

TIANJIN

SHANGHAI

CHONGQING

# CHINA

## Catherine Charley

MACDONALD YOUNG BOOKS

First published in 1994 by Simon & Schuster Young Books

First published in paperback in 1998 by Macdonald Young Books

Macdonald Young Books,
an imprint of Wayland Publishers Ltd
61 Western Road
Hove
East Sussex
BN3 1JD

Find Macdonald Young Books on the internet at:
http://www.myb.co.uk

| | |
|---|---|
| **Design** | Roger Kohn |
| **Editor** | Diana Russell |
| **DTP editor** | Helen Swansbourne |
| **Picture research** | Valerie Mulcahy |
| **Illustration** | Janos Marffy |
| **Calligraphy** | Leon Leung |
| **Consultant** | Ruth Cherrington |
| **Commissioning editor** | Debbie Fox |
| **1998 Consultant** | Liz Humphrey |

We are grateful to the following for permission
to reproduce photographs:
Front cover: Tony Stone Images *above,* Spectrum Colour
Library (D & J Heaton) *below*; Aspect picture Library, pages 9
(Peter Carmichael), 13 *below* (Ma Po Shum); Cepas Picture
Library/Nigel Blythe, pages 13 *above,* 22 *above,* 26 *below,* 34
*above*; Catherine Charley, page 21 *above* and *below*; China
National Tourist Office, page 8: Colorific!, pages 24 (Steve
Benbow), 34 *below* (Cary Wolinsky); Eye Ubiquitous/TRIP,
page 12; Sally and Richard Greenhill, page 23; Robert Harding
Picture Library, pages 20 and 25 (G & P Corrigan), 26/27, 29
(Peter Scholey), 32, 39 *above* (Gavin Hellier), 29 *below*; The
Image Bank/Chinese Photo Association, page 17; Magnum,
pages 18 *above* (Patrick Zachmann), 27 *below,* 33 and 38
*below* (Hiroji Kubota), 38 *above* (Michael K Nichols), 40 (Bruno
Barbey): Spectrum Colour Library, pages 35, 37
(D & J Heaton); Frank Spooner Pictures/Gamma, pages 14 (Remi
Benali), 18 *below* and 36 *above* (Anderson), 20 (Chip Hires);
Tony Stone Images, pages 22 *below* (Alain le Garsmeur), 31
(Julian Calder), 41, 43 (John Callahan); Sygma, pages 15 and
42 (Kees), 28 (G Rancinan), TRIP/Keith Cardwell, page 10
*above*; WWF Photolibrary, page 16 (Mauri Rautkari); Zefa,
page 10 *below*.

Special thanks to Laura Rivkin and all the staff at the
Great Britain–China Centre, London

Printed in Hong Kong by Wing King Tong Ltd

A CIP catalogue record for this book is available from the British Library

ISBN: 0 7500 2605 7

C
O
N
T
E
N
T
S

Words that are explained in the glossary are printed in
SMALL CAPITALS the first time they are mentioned in the text.

# INTRODUCTION

The only man-made object on Earth which can be seen from the Moon is the Great Wall of China, which stretches for 3,200 km across the north of China. China is the third largest country in the world (after Canada and the Russian Federation) and nearly a quarter of the world's population lives there.

The Chinese word for China is "Zhongguo", which means "Middle Kingdom". The ancient Chinese felt themselves to be the centre of the world. They had a highly developed civilization and for hundreds of years they traded silk and other goods with countries in Central Asia and Europe.

As Europe began to modernize in the 15th century, China was trying to preserve its old traditions and so its emperors closed the country to outsiders. In the 19th century, as China suffered from weak government and natural disasters like famines, Western nations took control of parts of the country including Hong Kong, which was taken over by the British.

In the early 20th century the COMMUNIST Party, established in 1921 and led by Mao Zedong, won the support of many of the Chinese people, especially in the countryside. In 1949, after a long civil war, the Communists defeated the Nationalist Party, led by Chiang Kaishek, and the People's Republic of China (PRC) was founded. For many years contact with CAPITALIST nations was discouraged. However, in the early 1980s, the government introduced the "Reform and Open Door Policy", which relaxed controls over industry and trade, and allowed more contact with other countries.

On July 1st 1997, Hong Kong was handed back to China from Britain under the terms of a treaty signed in 1898. Hong Kong is now a Special Administrative Region of China and has different laws to the rest of the country.

The next century will be a challenging time for the Chinese people.

◀ *Pan Pan the panda, the emblem of the Pan Asian Games held in Beijing in 1990. Holding the Games there was a sign to the world that China is no longer isolated.*

▶ *China now has many FREE MARKETS, where people do not have to buy and sell goods at prices set by the government.*

# CHINA AT A GLANCE

● Area: 9,571,300 square kilometres (excluding Taiwan and Hong Kong)
● Population of Mainland China (1996): 1,223,890,000
● Population of Hong Kong (1996): 6,061,000
● Population density of Mainland China: 126 people per sq km
● Capital: Beijing (Peking), population 10.78 m
● Other main cities: Shanghai 13.04 million; Tianjin 8.98 million; Chongqing 15.30 million; Shenyang 6.71 million; Wuhan 7.16 million; Guangzhou 6.56 million; Harbin 9.08 million; Chengdu 9.81 million; Xi'an 6.55 million; Nanjing 5.25 million; Dalian 5.37 million; Jinan 5.43 million; Changchun 6.77 million; Qingdao 6.8 million. (18 other cities have a population over 1 million)

● Highest mountain: Mount Everest ("Qomolangma"), 8,848 metres
● Official language: Mandarin Chinese
● Major religions: BUDDHISM, DAOISM, Confucianism, Islam, Christianity, Judaism
● Currency: Renminbi, written as RMB. Units: 1 Yuan = 10 Jiao = 100 Fen
● Economy: Agriculturally based. Most urban areas are highly industrialized
● Major resources: Large rivers, coal, iron ore, oil, gas, tin, tungsten, aluminium, other minerals
● Major products: Bicycles, paper, textiles, silk products, wheat, rice, tea, soya beans
● Environmental problems: Deforestation; grasslands turning into deserts; pollution of air, water and land near industrial areas and in cities

# THE LANDSCAPE

China covers almost 9.6 million square kilometres. The landscape descends like a staircase from the high mountain ranges of the west (the highest is the Himalayas), across the Tibet/Qinghai plateau and the lower mountain ranges and plains of eastern China, to the Pacific coast. Most of the mountain ranges run from west to east and the main rivers flow west to east, or north to south. Many of the ranges in the west are shared by countries bordering China, such as India, Nepal,

▲ *The limestone mountains in Guilin in southern China are famous for their unusual shape.*

▼ *The Himalayas in the south-west of Tibet are the highest mountains in the world. Every available piece of arable land in China is cultivated, even at this altitude.*

● China's lowest point is the Turpan Basin in the north-west: 154 metres below sea level.

● 25.9% of China lies above 3,000 metres.

● China has nearly 18,000 km of coastline.

● China covers the equivalent of an area stretching from northern Scandinavia to the north of Africa.

● There is just one time zone in China. It runs on Beijing time, so it can be light at midnight in Xinjiang region in the west.

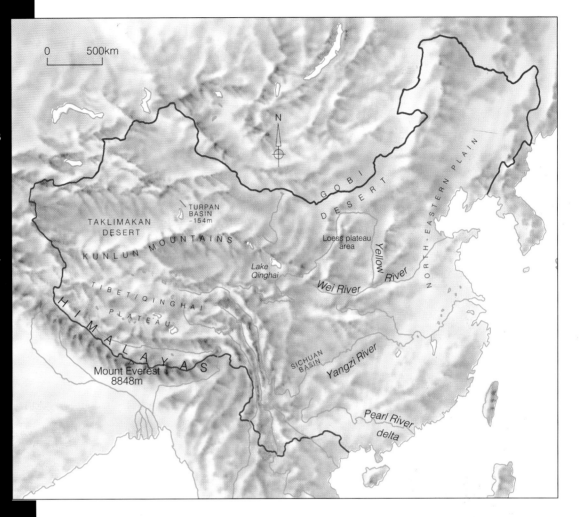

Pakistan and Russia.

The Tibet/Qinghai plateau, often called the "Roof of the World", is the largest highland region on Earth, with an area of over 2 million square kilometres. It covers 23% of China and is situated at an average altitude of 4,500 metres above sea level. North of this plateau, beyond the Kunlun

range, lies Xinjiang Autonomous Region, much of which is desert. Here is the Taklimakan Desert, one of the largest sand deserts in the world, stretching over 300,000 square kilometres. The Gobi Desert extends east from the Taklimakan Desert into Mongolia. It is separated from the Taklimakan by a series of oases.

Northern China's most important natural features are the Yellow River ("Huanghe"), named after the colour of the sediment it carries along its route, and the LOESS plateau. The river, 4,345 km long, flows roughly west to east, but makes a large loop, north and then south, through the fertile loess plateau before entering the North-Eastern Plain. One-third of China's

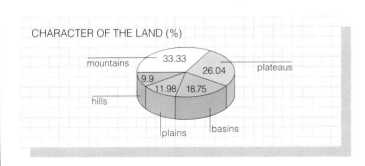

CHARACTER OF THE LAND (%)

mountains — 33.33

26.04 — plateaus

9.9

11.98 / 18.75

hills

plains — basins

population lives in this region. Chinese civilization began over 4,000 years ago in the valleys of the Yellow River and the Wei River, which joins it.

At 5,470 km, the Yangzi ("Changjiang") is China's longest river and the fourth longest in the world (after the Nile, Amazon and Mississippi). Changjiang means "Long River" in Chinese. Its source is west of Lake Qinghai on the Tibet/Qinghai plateau, from where it flows south and then eastwards before it reaches the Pacific at Shanghai.

The Yangzi is the official division between north and south China – in some cities which lie on both sides of the river, heating is provided for homes on the north side but not on the south, regardless of the temperature or weather.

Much of China south of the Yangzi is particularly mountainous. The middle and lower Yangzi plains, and the Pearl River delta ("Zhujiangkou") around Guangzhou, are where most of China's rice is grown. The Sichuan Basin is another great rice-growing area. This basin, which is surrounded by mountains, was formed from a huge prehistoric lake which left behind red soil deposits. It lies at an altitude of between 300 and 700 metres.

▼ **The Yellow River collects yellow-coloured silt as it flows through the loess regions of central and northern China.**

# CLIMATE AND WEATHER

◀ *This gorge and its caves are near the Turpan oasis in the desert region of north-west China.*

▼ *Tropical plants grow on Hainan Island off the coast of southern China. It is sometimes referred to as "China's Hawaii".*

The climate and weather in China are varied because of the country's size, landscape and location. China is so vast that it covers 30° of latitude from north to south and more than 60° of longitude from west to east. Bitterly cold winds from Siberia blow over the north at the same time as tropical plants grow in the south. In winter the temperature can be −20°C in the north-eastern city of Harbin near the Russian border, while at the same time it is +20°C in Haikou on Hainan Island in the far south.

Because of the varied landscape, even places near each other can have very different temperatures. In summer, the temperature in the northern part of the Tibetan highlands never reaches more than 10°C, while in the Turpan Basin just 1,000 km further north it can be as high as 47°C.

China's position between the large land mass of the Asian continent and the Pacific Ocean means the climate is affected by the cycle of the monsoon winds, caused by the temperature difference between the land and the sea. In the winter, bitterly cold dry winds blow from the interior of the continent over west and north China. Sometimes the winds bring dust from the desert and the loess regions. Winter in the south is milder, but there can be spells of cold, wet weather if winds move inland from the sea.

In the summer, warm moist winds enter southern China, making it hot and humid and bringing rain. These winds usually

▲ *The Ice Lantern Festival is held in the north-eastern city of Harbin from January to March every year. Buildings and other sculptures are made entirely from ice, and coloured lanterns are hung up inside them.*

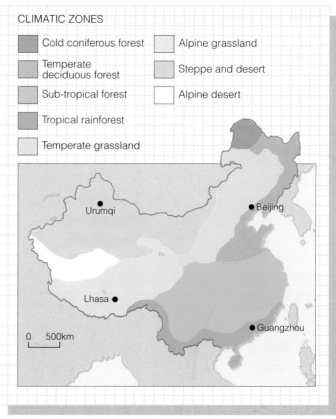

CLIMATIC ZONES

- Cold coniferous forest
- Temperate deciduous forest
- Sub-tropical forest
- Tropical rainforest
- Temperate grassland
- Alpine grassland
- Steppe and desert
- Alpine desert

Urumqi
Beijing
Lhasa
Guangzhou

0   500km

carry rain into the rest of China, but the pattern is irregular. If the winds move too quickly towards north China the central regions can suffer drought and floods occur in the north. Alternatively, if the winds meet northern air currents they will drop all their rain in central China and the northern regions might experience drought.

For centuries the Chinese have been building irrigation systems, canals, dikes and dams to try and control the water supply and prevent flooding. However,

## KEY FACTS

● On average the temperature drops 5–6°C for every 1,000 metres of altitude.

● Kunming, the capital of Yunnan province, is known as "Spring City" as its climate is so good all year round.

● Chongqing, Wuhan and Nanjing are called "the three furnaces" by the Chinese, because of their long, hot and humid summers.

● Typhoons are likely to hit the south-east coast between June and September.

▲ *Many parts of China often suffer from bad flooding. In summer 1991, 200 million people in east central China were affected by widespread and serious floods.*

there are still many natural disasters. The Yellow River is known as "China's sorrow" because of the devastation caused when it floods. Over the centuries the silt carried by the Yellow River has built up, raising the river bed to a level that is higher than the land alongside it. Dikes have been built to prevent the river flooding, but if the volume of water is high these dikes do not work. The Yangzi River also floods badly.

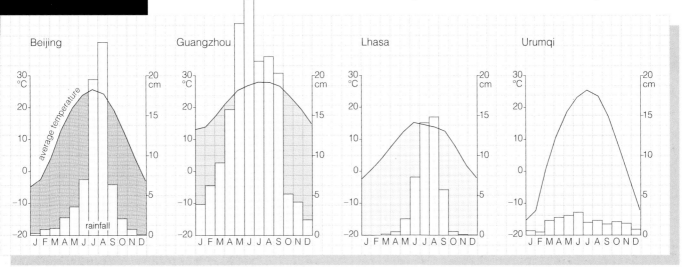

China has a large supply of natural resources. Coal provides 75% of its energy. The biggest coal deposits are in the north. Oil and natural gas also provide sources of energy. Many of the oil deposits are in the north-west and there are offshore oil fields in the East and South China Seas. It is believed that China has large reserves of oil both onshore and offshore, and various projects to explore these are under way, some of which are being carried out with foreign aid.

Most of China's water resources are in remote areas in the south and south-west. Water only provides 5% of China's energy, with various hydro-electric schemes bringing power to small, local areas. The largest dam is on the Yangzi at Gezhouba in Hubei province. A project to build the world's biggest dam and hydro-electric power station is now in progress in the Three Gorges in the middle section of the

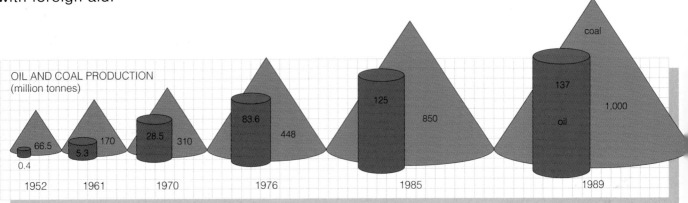

OIL AND COAL PRODUCTION
(million tonnes)

coal

| | | | | | | | coal |
| 0.4 | 66.5 | 5.3 | 170 | 28.5 | 310 | 83.6 | 448 | 125 | 850 | 137 oil | 1,000 |
| 1952 | | 1961 | | 1970 | | 1976 | | 1985 | | 1989 | |

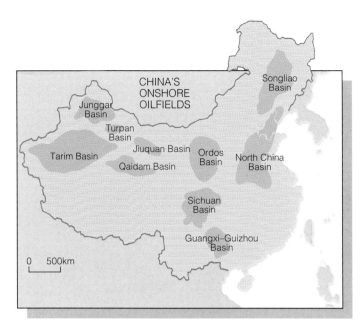

CHINA'S ONSHORE OILFIELDS

Songliao Basin

Junggar Basin

Turpan Basin

Jiuquan Basin

Tarim Basin

Qaidam Basin

Ordos Basin

North China Basin

Sichuan Basin

Guangxi–Guizhou Basin

0    500km

◄ *Coal is loaded on to barges on the Yangzi River at Wanxian in Sichuan province, to be transported to other parts of China.*

▼ *Drilling for oil in the desert in Xinjiang Autonomous Region in north-west China. China has both onshore and offshore oil reserves.*

Yangzi River. This project is proving controversial, as it involves moving 1 million people from their homes and flooding a large area of natural beauty. There are still enormous forests in the north-east and Tibet, providing timber for the paper industry.

China has abundant iron reserves, though they have a low iron content, and it is the world's principal producer of tungsten, which is used in light bulbs. There are large reserves of manganese and many other metals which are essential for the development of the steel industry. China also has deposits of lead, zinc, mercury, antimony, bauxite, silver, gold, aluminium, uranium and platinum.

The main problem is finding the best way to exploit the country's natural resources. Most are found in remote regions, far away from the industrial areas of central and eastern China. The hostile landscape means it is difficult and expensive to build transportation links.

## KEY FACTS

● China has deposits of most of the world's minerals.
● China is the world's largest coal producer.
● On the grasslands of Inner Mongolia, wind power supplies electricity for electric fences to prevent stock from roaming.
● When completed, the Three Gorges Dam will be the biggest dam in the world, generating up to 18,000MW of hydroelectricity.

# ★✦ POPULATION

Today, over 1.2 billion people live in China, more than in any other country in the world. The population has expanded rapidly since the 1950s. To stop it rising more steeply, in 1980 the government introduced a policy that limits most couples to having only one child. Despite this, it is estimated that the population will be over 1.3 billion by the beginning of the 21st century.

The One Child Policy is controversial because the Chinese traditionally have large families. In the cities most couples have followed the policy, but in the countryside people want more than one child. They particularly want a son to work on the land, keep the family name going and look after them in their old age. In the countryside, the One Child Policy has now been relaxed slightly.

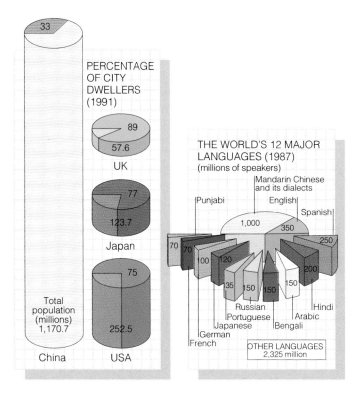

PERCENTAGE
OF CITY
DWELLERS
(1991)

89
57.6
UK

77
123.7
Japan

75
252.5
USA

Total population (millions)
1,170.7
China

33

THE WORLD'S 12 MAJOR LANGUAGES (1987)
(millions of speakers)

Mandarin Chinese and its dialects

Punjabi
English
Spanish
1,000
350
250
70
70
100
120
200
35
150
150
150
Russian
Hindi
Portuguese
Arabic
Japanese
Bengali
German
French

OTHER LANGUAGES
2,325 million

# KEY FACTS

● 22% of the world's population live in China.
● 51.03% of the population are male, 49.97% are female.
● Since 1949 average life expectancy has risen from 40 to about 70 years.
● In 1980 there were an estimated 15-20 million people of Chinese race living outside China, Taiwan and Hong Kong.
● Sichuan is China's most densely populated province.
● In Shanghai there are 2,000 inhabitants per sq km. In Tibet there are 1.5.
● The number of cities and towns in the Pearl River delta area in Guangdong province has increased from 33 in 1978 to 114 in 1986.

◀ **The streets of Shanghai are some of the most crowded in China. Shanghai's population has increased from 5 million in 1948 to over 13 million in 1996.**

◀ **There are posters throughout China encouraging couples to have only one child. China's population has grown from 540 million in 1949 to over 1.2 billion in 1996.**

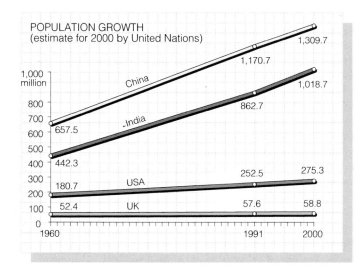

POPULATION GROWTH
(estimate for 2000 by United Nations)

1,000 million

China
657.5
1,170.7
1,309.7

India
442.3
862.7
1,018.7

USA
180.7
252.5
275.3

UK
52.4
57.6
58.8

1960
1991
2000

Half of the population in China is under 30 years of age, but living standards and medical conditions have improved over the last 40 years and people are now living longer. About 80% of people live in the east and south-east, on about a fifth of the total land. The government does not encourage people to move from the countryside to the cities, or from one city to another.

## CITIES AND COUNTRYSIDE

About 33% of people live in cities, towns and rural townships (new developments in the countryside). The cities are mainly situated in the east of the country and 32 of them have populations over 1 million. They are all growing. The current figures for cities do not reflect the fact that many people from the countryside are moving there without government permission, in the hope of finding work. Towns are also growing and the rural townships have developed since the late 1970s, as the government's economic changes have allowed small industries in areas where

*The Tibetan people live in the west of China. They are very religious and regard the Dalai Lama, who has lived in exile in India since 1959, as their leader.*

most people used to work on the land.

Some 67% of Chinese people live in the countryside. They are mainly farmers and peasants. As it is such a large country, their homes and life-styles vary. During the cold winters in northern China peasants might sleep, eat and sit on a "kang", a platform of loose clay bricks, which is heated by the small wood-burning stove where they do their cooking. In contrast, in the warm south-west some country people live in straw houses built on stilts.

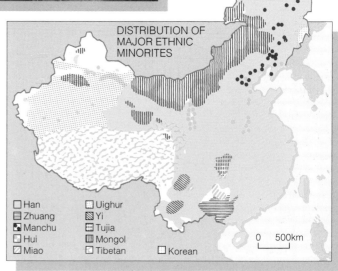

DISTRIBUTION OF MAJOR ETHNIC MINORITES

☐ Han
☷ Zhuang
◪ Manchu
☐ Hui
☐ Miao
☐ Uighur
◩ Yi
▦ Tujia
Ⅲ Mongol
☐ Tibetan
☐ Korean

0    500km

### LANGUAGE

The Chinese language is spoken in different dialects throughout the country, though the written forms are the same. The standard form of spoken Chinese is Mandarin, based on a northern dialect from the Beijing area. Cantonese is spoken in the area around Guangzhou.

### THE MINORITY NATIONALITIES

Approximately 92% of the people in China are Han Chinese, whom we would regard as typical Chinese. The rest are of different ethnic origins, for example the Tibetans and the Koreans. There are 55 of these groups, totalling about 70 million people. The Chinese call these people

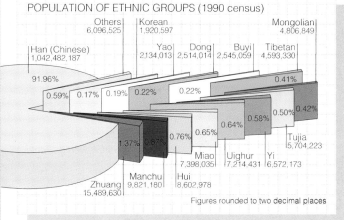

POPULATION OF ETHNIC GROUPS (1990 census)

Others 6,096,525
Korean 1,920,597
Mongolian 4,806,849
Han (Chinese) 1,042,482,187
Yao 2,134,013
Dong 2,514,014
Buyi 2,545,059
Tibetan 4,593,330
91.96%
0.41%
0.59%
0.17%
0.19%
0.22%
0.22%
0.42%
0.50%
0.58%
0.64%
0.65%
0.76%
1.37%
0.87%
Tujia 5,704,223
Miao 7,398,035
Uighur 7,214,431
Yi 6,572,173
Zhuang 15,489,630
Manchu 9,821,180
Hui 8,602,978

Figures rounded to two decimal places

◀ *The Uighurs are a Moslem people who live in the north-west of China in Xinjiang Autonomous Region. Their language is closely related to Turkish and they write in Arabic script.*

◀ *1.6 million Bai people live in Yunnan province in south-west China. There are 21 other minority groups in this province.*

the minority nationalities. They usually have a different language, different customs and a different religion to the Han Chinese. They are scattered over 50% of the territory, though they tend to be concentrated in the border and mountain regions.

Some minorities, such as the Tibetans and the Uighurs, want independence. The government has encouraged the Han Chinese to move to minority regions, with the result that they now often outnumber the minority peoples in some of these areas. The One Child Policy is not applied as strictly among the minority groups.

# ▣ DAILY LIFE

Both urban and rural areas of China are changing and becoming more modern. Since the early 1980s, a growing number of Western goods and influences have been affecting people's lives. For example, in 1984 only 3% of Beijing households had fridges, but by 1989 the number had risen to 60%.

## FAMILY LIFE

In the past most people in cities and towns were assigned to jobs for life. Accommodation usually came with the job. Things are beginning to change; students and others can apply for jobs, while in some cities and countryside areas people are now allowed to buy or build their own properties. Because there are housing shortages in the cities, many people live with their parents.

Traditionally, the family plays a very important part in Chinese life, and the Communist Party has reinforced this idea. Chinese people have a lot of respect for older and more senior people.

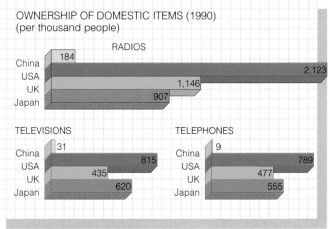

OWNERSHIP OF DOMESTIC ITEMS (1990)
(per thousand people)

RADIOS
China 184
USA 2,123
UK 1,146
Japan 907

TELEVISIONS
China 31
USA 815
UK 435
Japan 620

TELEPHONES
China 9
USA 789
UK 477
Japan 555

◀ *Most people in the cities live in flats. Their homes usually have no hot running water and they often have to use a communal shower block.*

▶ *Tea-houses are popular places for men to meet and chat.*

◀ *In the countryside, people often play Chinese chess on the street, with spectators watching and encouraging. Other games include cards and ping pong (played on a concrete table, using bricks for a net).*

## EDUCATION

Schooling is supposed to be compulsory for nine years, but it is not available to all children in remote areas. In addition, farmers and peasants often take their children out of school early as they want them to help work on the land. They are also less likely to educate their daughters. About 22% of the population is illiterate or semi-illiterate, but this is a great improvement on the figure of 80% in 1949.

In the cities, many young children go to all-day kindergartens, as their mothers work full time. Otherwise, children start school at the age of six and go to primary school for five or six years, then there is junior middle school for three years and senior middle school for two or three years. There are exams at the end of primary school and at the end of junior and senior middle school. There are also "key schools", which provide the best education for entry to universities, and parents in the cities are keen to send their children to these schools. Only a small percentage of pupils go on to higher education.

The school day runs from 8 am to noon and from 2 pm to 4 pm. Pupils have homework as well. There are two terms in the year. The first lasts from September to January, with a month off for the Spring Festival holiday. The second is from February or March to June, with two months' summer holiday.

## LEISURE

The Chinese used to work a six day week, but this was recently changed officially to five days (Monday to Friday). Sunday is the day when everyone in the cities goes to the parks.

## KEY FACTS

● The Chinese place the family name first. In the name Wu Xiaopei, the family name is Wu. Outside the family, people are usually called by the family name.

● The mother keeps her maiden name when she marries; a child takes the father's family name.

● The given name usually has a meaning. For instance, Xiaopei means Little Jewel.

● In 1982, 0.6% of the population graduated from higher education. In 1990 the figure was 1.4%.

● The legal age for men to marry is 22. For women it is 20.

● A factory often has its own health centre, and perhaps a small hospital too.

● In 1989, China had 1,010 people per doctor, compared with 419 in the USA.

Because living conditions are often cramped, people carry out their leisure activities outside the home. These vary from traditional Chinese activities to modern Western ones; in the early morning old people do TAI JI QUAN in the parks and as they wait for buses, while in the evenings young people play pool on tables in the streets. Others gather to hear live traditional Chinese opera, or pop music on a tape recorder, or to join ballroom-dancing

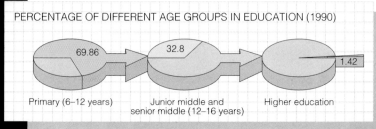

PERCENTAGE OF DIFFERENT AGE GROUPS IN EDUCATION (1990)

69.86    32.8    1.42

Primary (6–12 years)    Junior middle and senior middle (12–16 years)    Higher education

◀ *Physical exercise is an important part of the school curriculum. Pupils usually have to do 10 minutes of set exercises every morning before classes begin.*

▼ *A boy practises the traditional way to write Chinese characters with a brush and ink.*

classes. In the countryside travelling street theatre, weight-lifting and open-air film shows are popular. Men often gather in tea-houses to drink tea, chat and smoke. Some 70% of Chinese men smoke and this is a growing health problem.

Discos and karaoke are popular among young people, while eating with family and friends has always been a social pastime for all ages. The lottery has become very popular in Guangzhou. In the cities people keep birds and goldfish as pets. Goldfish are supposed to be lucky. The most popular sports are table tennis and football.

## RELIGION AND CULTURE

Officially religion is allowed in China, but it is not encouraged. Communists do not approve of religion and in the 1960s and

一 YE (1)
二 ER (2)
三 SAN (3)
四 SI (4)
五 WU (5)
六 LIU (6)
七 QI (7)
八 BA (8)
九 JIU (9)
十 SHI (10)

日 RI (sun)
月 YUE (moon)
山 SHAN (mountain)
木 MU (tree or wood)
人 REN (man or person)
子 ZI (child or seed)
中 国 ZHONGGUO (China)
ZHONG (middle)
GUO (country)

◀▲ *The Chinese have no alphabet. They write using diagrams called characters. Words are made up of one or more characters. There are over 60,000 characters in the Chinese language. About 4,000 are needed for a basic level of literacy and to read a newspaper. Children have to learn 400–500 characters a year at school.*

1970s many religious places in China were closed. The government has recently become more tolerant and people are beginning to set up family shrines again, where they can worship their ancestors. Many temples, mosques and churches have re-opened.

The main religion in China is Buddhism. Daoism and ancestor worship are other traditional beliefs. There are also temples dedicated to Confucius, a Chinese scholar and philosopher who lived 2,500 years ago. He drew up strict rules for life which included respecting elders and seniors. Islam, Christianity and Judaism are also practised in China.

Both modern Western medical techniques and traditional Chinese medicine are used in China. In Chinese medicine the belief is that the whole body should be balanced if it is to work properly. Medicines are made from a mixture of herbs. In acupuncture, needles are applied to specific points on the body

▼ *Spectators watch a Dragon Dance during the Spring Festival, the Chinese New Year. This is the main holiday of the year and many people travel long distances to be with their families.*

### FESTIVALS AND HOLIDAYS

| | |
|---|---|
| January 1 | **NEW YEAR**<br>Public holiday. |
| Jan/Feb<br>(moveable) | **SPRING FESTIVAL**<br>**(CHINESE NEW YEAR)**<br>3 day public holiday. |
| March 8 | **WOMEN'S DAY**<br>1/2 day holiday for women. |
| April 5 | **QING MING**<br>Remembering the dead. |
| May 1 | **WORKERS' DAY**<br>Public holiday.<br>People have free entry to parks. |
| May/June<br>(moveable) | **DRAGON BOAT FESTIVAL** |
| June 1 | **CHILDREN'S DAY** |
| August 1 | **ARMY DAY**<br>To show respect for the Army. |
| Sept/Oct<br>(moveable) | **MOON FESTIVAL**<br>Like a harvest festival; held at the full moon.<br>"Mooncakes" are eaten. |
| October 1 | **NATIONAL DAY**<br>2 day public holiday.<br>Celebrates the day when Mao Zedong proclaimed the People's Republic in 1949. |

# KEY FACTS

● The Chinese drink tea with no milk or sugar.
● Throughout China, people keep boiled water in thermos flasks for drinking, as tap water is not safe to drink.

◄**Two men practise Tai Ji Quan outside the walls of the Forbidden City, the old imperial palace in the centre of Beijing.**

▼**Visitors to Sanyuangong shrine in Guangdong province. After a period of repression, religion in China is now on the increase again.**

▶ *The different regions of China have their own traditional styles of opera. The stories are based on old legends and events in history. The make-up and clothes of a theatrical character are very important. A red beard in Beijing Opera, for example, means courage. The actors paint their own faces and this can sometimes take up to 3 hours. The flags on the back of this character from Beijing Opera show that he is a General.*

to help ease and cure ailments. Qi Gong is a form of creating high energy through meditation, while Tai Ji Quan and martial arts are also based on meditation principles.

## SOCIAL PROBLEMS

The economic changes in China mean that people's lives are altering. A large gap is developing between the incomes of those working in the state sector, like teachers and state factory employees, and the owners of new businesses. Inflation is high. The crime rate has been low for many years, but it is now growing. Women have been officially equal in law since 1949, but in practice they still do most of the housework and have less important jobs. Divorce is difficult to obtain, but the rates are beginning to rise.

# RULE AND LAW

◀ *The National People's Congress meets in the Great Hall of the People in Tiananmen Square in Beijing, which was built in 10 months in 1958–9. It is opposite the old palace of the Chinese emperors.*

In 1911 the last Chinese Emperor was deposed and a republic was established. After a period of civil war and changing governments, the Nationalist Party was defeated by the Communists, who formed the People's Republic of China in 1949, headed by Chairman Mao Zedong. The Chinese Communist Party (CCP) has ruled China ever since, except for the island of Taiwan (which used to be governed from the mainland), where the Nationalists set up the Republic of China (ROC).

There are various governing bodies in the People's Republic of China, at both national and local level. They all exist alongside the CCP structure. The National People's Congress (NPC) is the central parliament and it meets for two or three weeks once a year. Representatives are elected every five years by the local congresses all over China, which represent the 22 provinces, 5 autonomous regions

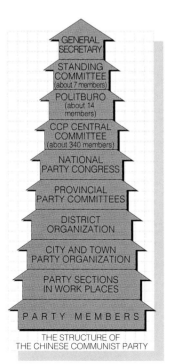

THE STRUCTURE OF THE CHINESE COMMUNIST PARTY

◀ *Members of the Chinese Communist Party (CCP), China's most important governing body, are active at every level of society.*

▶ *Most representatives in the National People's Congress are also Communist Party members.*

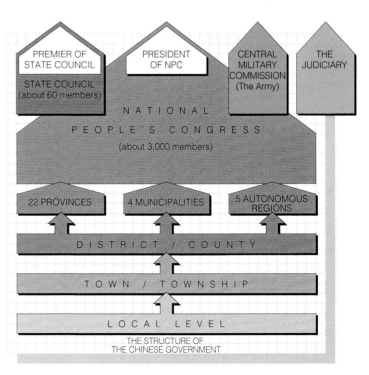

THE STRUCTURE OF THE CHINESE GOVERNMENT

*In 1989 people filled Tiananmen Square for several weeks, in peaceful demonstrations to demand political reforms. On 4 June the government sent in soldiers and tanks against them. Many were killed.*

▼ *The death penalty exists for various crimes, including murder, rape and some political offences.*

and 4 municipalities. The autonomous regions are areas where large groupings of minority people live, for example Ningxia and Guizhou. One member of the State Council represents the Special Administrative Region of Hong Kong.

The NPC discusses and approves plans for the national economy and decides whether to go to war. It selects the main officials and groups to run the country. The country is controlled by these and by other influential people, who are often retired from all official posts - like Deng Xiaoping, former Chairman of the Communist Party and former Chairman of the Central Military Commission (the Army), until his death in 1997.

The top government posts are all held by members of the CCP. The Standing Committee and Politburo of the CCP are the most powerful bodies in the country and deal with all major issues. Senior army personnel are also often appointed to government positions.

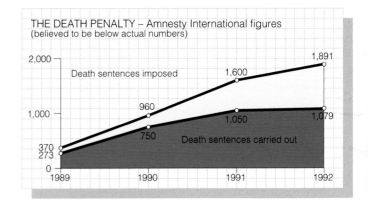

THE DEATH PENALTY – Amnesty International figures
(believed to be below actual numbers)

The CCP has to approve all election candidates. Many of the positions in government are filled by people who are appointed to the posts rather than being elected. This system sometimes causes dissatisfaction, with people demanding freer elections and more choice over who governs the country. This was one of the main causes of the protests in Tiananmen Square in the spring of 1989, which led to the government sending in troops against the protesters.

### ARTICLE 1 OF THE CONSTITUTION OF THE PEOPLE'S REPUBLIC OF CHINA:

"The People's Republic of China is a socialist state under the people's democratic dictatorship led by the working class and based on the alliance of workers and peasants.

The socialist system is the basic system of the People's Republic of China. Disruption of the socialist system by any organization or individual is prohibited."

▼ *National Day parade in Beijing. China's army is called the People's Liberation Army (PLA). It has about 3 million members.*

## KEY FACTS

● Beijing means Northern Capital ('Bei" = North, 'Jing' = Capital).
● Nanjing, which was a capital city in the past, means Southern Capital
● Article 48 of the Constitution states that women are equal with men in all spheres of life.
● In 1997 the most senior woman in Chinese government was the Minister of Foreign Trade, Mrs Wu Yi.
● There are 1,936 countries in China.
● Many of the police force are armed with electric batons.
● The number of crimes being committed by young people is increasing.

# FOOD AND FARMING

Rice is the staple food for most people in China, especially in the south. In the north and west it is too dry to grow rice, so people there also use wheat flour to make noodles and bread. All grain crops are rationed and heavily subsidized. Meat is only eaten a couple of times a week, usually pork (except for the Moslems) or chicken. People eat mutton more in western China, where they graze sheep on the hills.

▼ *Most farmers in China use traditional methods to plant and tend their crops. They push tractors by hand and use oxen to pull ploughs.*

The Chinese eat fish from both rivers and the sea, and there are fish farms in the east. As China covers such a large area, there is a great diversity of fruit and vegetables, ranging from melons to apples and from Chinese cabbages to peppers.

Traditionally, the Han Chinese do not eat much dairy produce, because in the past they used all the available land for growing crops. Now imports of animal cereals are increasing to feed the growing number of dairy animals that are being kept.

Chinese cooking is famous the world over and there are many regional variations in dishes. In the north of China "jiaozi", or

# KEY FACTS

- In all but 3 provinces, municipalities or autonomous regions, industry accounts for at least a third of the local income.
- In 1995, the Chinese provinces with the highest industrial output were Jiangsu (Y1,181,286 million), Guangdong (Y953,542 million) and Shandong (Y845,632 million).
- Toys, games and sporting goods accounted for 14.4% of the USA's imports from China in 1992. Garments accounted for 17.4% and footwear for 13.2%.

dumplings, are made by family and friends for the Spring Festival and other gatherings, while in the south tiny flavoured snacks called "dim sum" are popular. Sichuan and Hunan provinces are famous for hot, spicy food. Mealtimes are a very important part of family life. Families get together, and adults and children even travel home for lunch from work and school if they can.

China is still mainly an agricultural country, although only 11% of the land is suitable for growing crops. The most intensively farmed land is in the east and centre. Some land is very productive, such

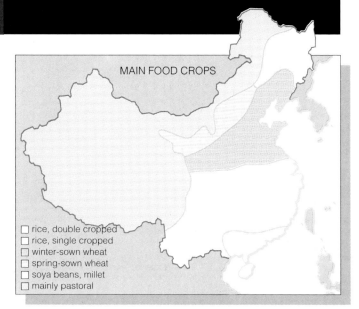

MAIN FOOD CROPS

- ☐ rice, double cropped
- ☐ rice, single cropped
- ☐ winter-sown wheat
- ☐ spring-sown wheat
- ☐ soya beans, millet
- ☐ mainly pastoral

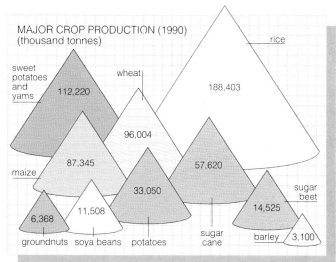

MAJOR CROP PRODUCTION (1990)
(thousand tonnes)

rice 188,403
sweet potatoes and yams 112,220
wheat 96,004
maize 87,345
sugar cane 57,620
potatoes 33,050
sugar beet 14,525
soya beans 11,508
groundnuts 6,368
barley 3,100

▶ *Planting a rice paddy field in Guilin, south China. In some areas farmers can harvest a rice crop two or three times a year.*

Many shops in China still use abacuses to calculate the cost of purchases

To prepare a traditional meal, the food is cut into small pieces and cooked in a WOK. The different dishes are placed on the table for all to share.

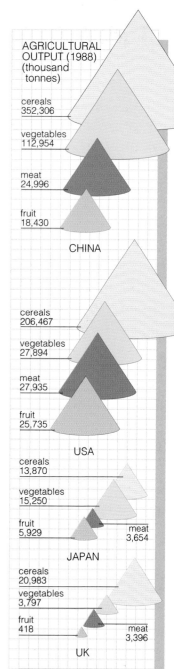

AGRICULTURAL OUTPUT (1988) (thousand tonnes)

**CHINA**
cereals 352,306
vegetables 112,954
meat 24,996
fruit 18,430

**USA**
cereals 206,467
vegetables 27,894
meat 27,935
fruit 25,735

**JAPAN**
cereals 13,870
vegetables 15,250
fruit 5,929
meat 3,654

**UK**
cereals 20,983
vegetables 3,797
fruit 418
meat 3,396

as the Sichuan Basin, and can produce two or three harvests a year. At present China can just about manage to feed all its people, but the continually increasing population means it might not be able to do so for much longer. Most farming is still done in the traditional way. Apart from rice and wheat, agricultural products include soya beans, barley, sorghum, oats, potatoes, tea, oil seed crops and sugar-cane. Cotton and rubber are important industrial crops.

Between 1958 and 1978 all food in China was grown by COMMUNES and had to be sold to the government at a fixed price. Since 1978 individual farmers and peasants have been allowed to rent land. After selling a certain amount of produce at a set price to the government, they can take the rest to the new free markets, where they sell it for whatever price people are prepared to pay. Some farmers have made a lot of money over the last few years and are building themselves new houses, which are using up valuable farm land.

China's industries are chiefly situated in the east and central parts of the country. Many of the northern industrial cities are near sites of coal and iron ore. When the Communists came to power in 1949, one of their main aims was to speed up industrialization. They favoured heavy industries such as steel works, and between 1952 and 1989 annual steel output increased from 1.4 million tonnes to 61.2 million tonnes. Today, while these industries are still important, there is a shift to light industries, such as the manufacture of consumer goods (fridges, TVs, etc), and to service industries such as banking and insurance.

This reflects the enormous changes currently taking place in China's trade and industry. Until recently all places of work, known as "work units", were run by the state and controlled by the Communist Party. Since the early 1980s, the government has freed some companies and factories from state control and allowed private individuals to set up businesses. Foreigners are now allowed to invest in China.

## SPECIAL ECONOMIC ZONES

Special Economic Zones (SEZs) are areas where Chinese people and foreigners are encouraged to invest and start businesses without the restrictions imposed by the Communist system in the rest of China. The first four SEZs - Shenzhen, Zhuhai,

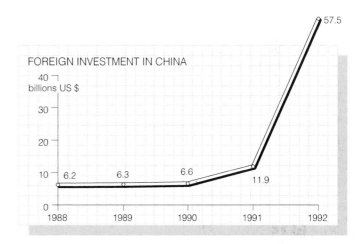

FOREIGN INVESTMENT IN CHINA

57.5

40
billions US $

30

20

10    6.2        6.3         6.6

0                                         11.9

1988      1989      1990      1991      1992

▶*Shanghai's stock exchange opened in 1990 as part of the government's economic development policies. A second stock exchange opened in Shenzhen in 1991.*

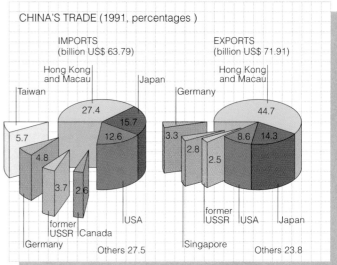

CHINA'S TRADE (1991, percentages )

IMPORTS
(billion US$ 63.79)

EXPORTS
(billion US$ 71.91)

▲ *Chinese factories are now producing consumer goods, such as televisions, after years of concentrating on heavy industry.*

Shantou and Xiamen - were declared in 1980. Hainan island was added in 1988. Up to 1997, 14 other coastal cities had been opened up to foreign investment. Many foreign companies work jointly with Chinese businesses. Guangdong Province, where there are two SEZs, is one of the fastest developing areas in Asia.

## IMPORTS AND EXPORTS

Some of China's most important exports are garments, cotton yarn, woven fabrics, machinery, electronic products, crude petroleum and refined petroleum products. China is now a major centre for assembling parts for computers and other industries. All these goods bring foreign currency into the country, which China can use to buy equipment for its modernization programme. Major imports in 1990 included materials and parts for processing, machinery and electronic products, steel products and fertilizers.

★SPECIAL ECONOMIC ZONES

▲ *Shenzhen is one of China's Special Economic Zones (SEZs), where incentives such as low taxes encourage Chinese and foreigners to develop businesses.*

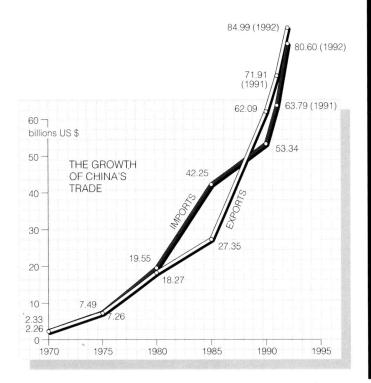

THE GROWTH
OF CHINA'S
TRADE

60
billions US $

50

40

30

20

10

2.33
2.26
0

1970    1975    1980    1985    1990    1995

84.99 (1992)
80.60 (1992)
71.91 (1991)
63.79 (1991)
62.09
53.34
42.25
27.35
19.55
18.27
7.49
7.26

IMPORTS
EXPORTS

◀ *Tourism is developing in China. The Great Wall is one of the most famous sites from the country's long history which all visitors want to see. It was originally begun by the first Emperor over 2,000 years ago, when he linked up the existing walls of different kingdoms to prevent invasions from the north.*

## EFFECTS OF THE NEW POLICIES

As well as these changes in large industries, the new government policies have made it possible for individuals or small businesses to make a great deal of money from activities such as selling goods in the free markets. They deal in everything from bananas to motor-bikes and from kitchen utensils to underwear.

Some people say that the new policies mean China is becoming more like a capitalist country and it can no longer call itself a Communist country. Deng Xiaoping, who was behind the push for economic reforms, has said, "It doesn't matter what colour the cat is, black or white, as long as it catches the mouse."

# ★ TRANSPORT

Despite its size and difficult terrain, public transport in China is fairly good. Most people travel long distances by train rather than bus or aeroplane, as the roads are poor and flying is expensive. There is a railway network to all provinces except Tibet, although this is being constructed, and special railways serve factories and mines. It takes 28 hours to travel the 2,313 kilometres from Beijing to Guangzhou by train.

▲ *The bicycle is the main form of private transport in China.*

◄ *60 people can sleep in a train's "hard sleeper" carriage. The bunks are in groups of 6 and open out on to the corridor. During the day people sit on the bottom bunks, play cards and chat.*

## KEY FACTS

● During the wet season, the Yangzi River, one of China's main transport systems, is navigable by 15,000 tonne ships as far as Wuhan (more than 1,000 km inland).
● Mainland Chinese airlines carried a total of 51,170,000 passengers in 1995 compared with 16,596,000 in 1990.
● In 1994, the total length of the railway network was 54,616 km.

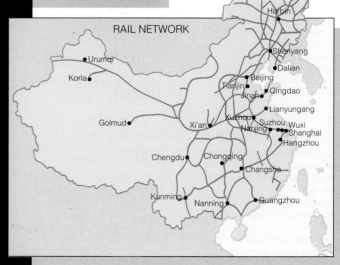

RAIL NETWORK

Urumqi · Korla · Golmud · Chengdu · Kunming · Nanning · Xi'an · Chongqing · Changsha · Guangzhou · Harbin · Shenyang · Dalian · Beijing · Tianjin · Jinan · Qingdao · Lianyungang · Xuzhou · Suzhou · Wuxi · Nanjing · Shanghai · Hangzhou

NUMBER OF BICYCLES AND CARS (millions, mid-1980s)

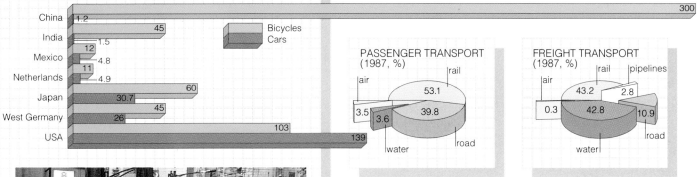

| | Bicycles | Cars |
|---|---|---|
| China | 300 | 1.2 |
| India | 45 | 1.5 |
| Mexico | 12 | 4.8 |
| Netherlands | 11 | 4.9 |
| Japan | 60 | 30.7 |
| West Germany | 45 | 26 |
| USA | 103 | 139 |

PASSENGER TRANSPORT (1987, %)

air 3.5
water 3.6
road 39.8
rail 53.1

FREIGHT TRANSPORT (1987, %)

air 0.3
water 42.8
road 10.9
rail 43.2
pipelines 2.8

The average train ride in China lasts 10 hours. More than 70% of towns and villages are connected to the main road system. Rivers and canals are used to take passengers and freight inland.

In the cities the buses are cheap and plentiful, but always over-crowded. Beijing and Tianjin both have underground train systems, built in the early 1980s. A new airport in Hong Kong, which was started before the handover, will open in 1998.

◀ *Road congestion is becoming serious in some cities. The number of vehicles on the road almost doubled between 1990 and 1995.*

▶ *The CAAC (Civil Aviation Administration of China) licenses and operates China's airlines. Air traffic is currently expanding by 30% a year.*

*◀ The pulp and paper industry causes a sixth of the water pollution in China. This could rapidly increase, as currently the amount of paper used per person in the country is very low. The tanning industry is another serious source of water pollution.*

China already has environmental problems, which seem likely to worsen as the country modernizes and becomes richer. Currently in China an average of 1 tonne of coal is used per person per year, ten times less than the figure in the USA. If China starts to use the same amount of coal as the West does, this will have serious effects on global warming.

Industry is responsible for about 70% of the pollution in China. Many industrial cities suffer from acid rain and most rivers passing through major cities are severely polluted. Chinese industries often use large amounts of raw materials, including water and energy, in relation to their output.

In an attempt to get as much produce as possible from the small amount of crop-growing land, some areas have been farmed too intensively and often pesticides and fertilizers have been over-used. In addition, the growing population in the cities is forcing developments to be built on valuable farm land.

On the northern grasslands of China the desert is expanding, because over-grazing has left too little grass to hold the soil in place. Cutting down too many trees has meant that the forests in western Sichuan, where the giant panda lives, are getting smaller, despite the creation of several nature reserves. Other animals, such as bears and tigers, are under threat because of their use in traditional Chinese medicine.

The government is aware of the problems and has set up the Natural Environmental Protection Agency (NEPA) to try and do something about them. One scheme it has organized is a massive tree-planting campaign, known as "The Green Wall" campaign, to try and prevent farming land in northern China from being washed or blown away. The government is also trying to reduce pollution from some industries, such as coal and oil producers and manufacturers of chemicals, metals, food and building materials.

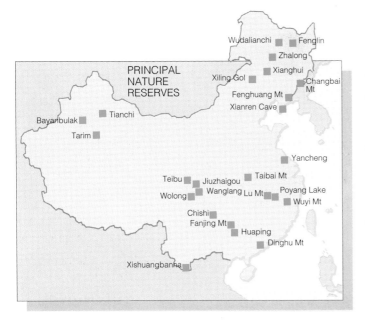

PRINCIPAL
NATURE
RESERVES

◀ *There are over 350 nature reserves in China.*

▼ *The giant panda is the symbol of the World Wide Fund for Nature. It only lives in the forests of western Sichuan province and eats a specific type of bamboo shoot which grows there. Because these forests are being cut down, there are now only 700 giant pandas left in the wild.*

# KEY FACTS

● In one single reserve in Sichuan province there are 4,000 species of native plants – more than in the whole of Europe.

● In many cities coal briquettes are burnt for fuel, which means coal dust adds to the pollution.

● Yunnan province has over 2,000 plant species which can be used in medicines.

● Many village communities tip their plant, animal and human waste, together with water, into air-tight concrete containers. The mixture ferments and produces methane gas, which is used for fuel.

# THE FUTURE

The People's Republic of China is changing very quickly. The new economic reforms are bringing prosperity to some people, but not to others. In particular, unemployment is rising and causing poverty in the cities. Also, as technology increases, there will inevitably be growing unemployment in the countryside. The challenge for the government now is to continue economic development without causing too many problems in society.

China is a huge and diverse country. Economic developments are increasing the differences between the backward areas and those that are more advanced. In addition, the Tibetans in the west would like to break away to form their own country, while the Uighurs in the north-west are also starting to call for greater independence.

One of China's major problems is the steady growth of its population. The government is trying to limit the population

▲ *Over the last 10 years Western influences have affected all aspects of life in China. A trip to the new McDonald's in Beijing is now part of the sight-seeing trip for a family visiting from the countryside.*

growth through the One Child Policy. This will mean that in the next decade, there will be more elderly than young people. The Chinese are also concerned that all these single children will be spoilt by their families.

China is moving forward into an exciting new century. Greater freedom and wealth have transformed Chinese society during the last decade, and the changes are set to continue. China will increasingly take advantage of Western technology whilst retaining its unique culture. Once again, China may become one of the most powerful countries in the world.

The Chinese people are used to being patient and looking ahead to the future. A Chinese saying states: "You have to water the seed to see the tree."

▼ *Hong Kong is a major capitalist economy, and a regional financial centre. It is also a gateway to mainland China for many international businesses. Now that it is part of Communist China, the maintenance of prosperity in Hong Kong over the next decade will be a key test for the Chinese government. They want to preserve Hong Kong as a support for the development of mainland China and to prove to the rest of the world that they can govern a world class economy.*

## KEY FACTS

● China is a nuclear power and has been testing weapons in the Taklimakan Desert.
● China has been launching satellites into space since 1970.
● Over the 1990s, the Chinese population will have increased by about 125 million people - equivalent to half the population of the USA.
● By the year 2035 more than a quarter of China's population will be over 65 years old.
● The island of Macau is being returned to China by Portugal in 1999.
● Mainland China would also like to regain control over Taiwan, which is currently an independent republic.

# FURTHER INFORMATION

- **GREAT BRITAIN-CHINA CENTRE**
15 Belgrave Square, London SW1X 8PS
E Mail: Contact@gbcc.org.uk
Has a library with information about China.
- **CHINESE EMBASSY CULTURAL SECTION**
11 West Heath Road, London NW3 7UX
Provides leaflets and audio-visual material on China.
- **(CTS) CHINA TRAVEL SERVICE**
24 Cambridge Circus, London WC2H 8HD
Has leaflet's on China regions.
- **MANCHESTER CHINESE ARTS CENTRE**
36 Charlotte Street, Manchester M1 4FD
Produces teaching packs on Chinese arts and culture.
- Many cities in the UK have a CHINESE COMMUNITY CENTRE. Try contacting your local centre to find out about the Chinese community in your area.

## BOOKS ABOUT CHINA
*China Today*, D C Money, Cambridge University Press 1987 (age 11–16)
*Focus on China*, Jessie Lim, Evans Brothers 1991 (age 8–11)

## ROMANIZATION
In this book Chinese characters are romanized (written in the alphabet used by Western countries) according to the form called "Pinyin", which is used by the PRC. The standard romanization used in Hong Kong and Taiwan is different.

| PINYIN | TRADITIONAL |
|---|---|
| Beijing | Peking |
| Guangzhou | Canton |
| Mao Zedong | Mao Tse'tung |
| Zhongguo (China) | Chung-kuo |
| Xinjiang | Sinkiang |
| Sichuan | Szechwan |
| Daoism | Taoism |

# GLOSSARY

**BUDDHISM**
A religion which originated in India in the 5th century BC and came to China in the 1st century AD.

**CAPITALISM**
An economic system in which individuals own businesses and keep the profits.

**COMMUNE**
A group of villages where the peasants shared and worked the land together. All produce had to be sold to the government at a set price.

**COMMUNISM**
An economic and political system in which private ownership is abolished and all industry is controlled by the state.

**DAOISM**
A Chinese religion and philosophy which teaches that people should live in harmony with nature.

**FREE MARKET**
A market where goods can be bought and sold at whatever price people are prepared to pay, often with some haggling.

**LOESS**
The accumulation of fine, light-coloured grains of clay or silt deposited by the wind.

**TAI JI QUAN**
A form of exercise and meditation.

**WOK**
A large metal pan, used to stir-fry food in Chinese cooking.

# INDEX

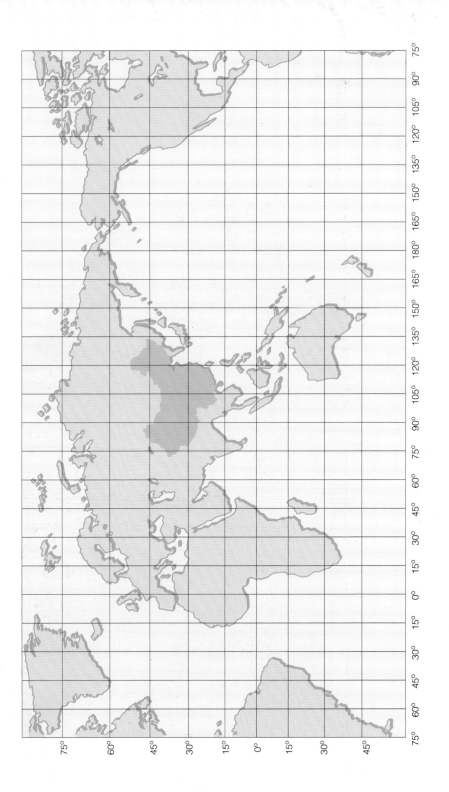

**In addition to China's 22 provinces, there are:**

**5 AUTONOMOUS REGIONS**

NEI MONGGOL (Inner Mongolia)
XIZANG (Tibet)
XINJIANG
GUANGXI
NINGXIA

**1 SPECIAL ADMINISTRATIVE REGION**

HONG KONG

**4 MUNICIPALITIES**

BEIJING
TIANJIN
SHANGHAI
CHONGQING